Poem… …,
Love and Death

Madeline Sharples

Cyberwit.net
HIG 45 Kaushambi Kunj, Kalindipuram
Allahabad - 211011 (U.P.) India
http://www.cyberwit.net
Tel: +(91) 9415091004
E-mail: info@cyberwit.net

Printed at Repro India Limited.

Contents

For Ben

Only suckling or holding you against
my belly and breasts would quiet you.
Not even your thumbs
(you didn't care which) eased your cries
in those first few months.
When finally the crying stopped you emerged
determined to take on the world.
That Benjamin, we called you.

"Look, I can ride a 2-wheeler
"and I'm only 3," you shouted
with pale hair like fine corn silk
flying and huge hazel eyes
seeing nothing but the road.

You lived your young life in competition
reading the most books,
writing the most journal pages,
earning the most As,
running the fastest 10K,
collecting the most Garbage Pail Kids
and hitting the best
backhand down the line.

You loved the pressure
It made you nervous
(I said excited)
It was your fuel
You had to be the best.

Your tennis consumed you and me
as we drove miles.
You in your trademark baseball cap
battled your opponents while
I battled freeway phobia.
Not quite 8, you overcame 1 to 6
in a second set tie break
to win your first championship trophy.
They called you "Iceman" as
you coolly walked off the court.

It was not all serious.
You wrote the scripts and then filmed
Andy, Dan, Cam, Josh or Brad
walking down the long hall,
gun in hand,
ready to pounce on the next victim
or pretend to throw him over the deck.
In every film someone went
over the deck.
For such a gentle, sweet boy,
you sure loved violence.

You also loved to mimic
McEnroe's serve,
Kline's "k-k-k-ken,"
Hoffman's "I'm an excellent driver,"
and the Three Amigos.
You made us snicker
when you called someone
an emma, a foof, a donkey, a nick
or cute and funny and silly and nice.

But I was most charmed when you
touched my face and said,
"Your cheeks are nice and soft, are mine?"
or "Come sleep with me for a minute"
when I would wake you
to get ready for school.
Little did I know that,
that early play acting
was practice for your passion.

I watched you with arms uplifted,
legs spread wide,
speaking in a loud, deep voice that comes
from the bottom of your belly.
Your presence filled the stage.
Your lean, firm body
enclosed in a skin-tight suit
the color of a ripe peach,
finger and toe nails painted wine red
like the deep stain on your lips,
your hair sticking up like the spokes of a bike
you did a cartwheel across the floor.
You found where you most want to be.

As your high school teacher said,
"You have the world on a string."
Keep a tight hold
it's all yours for the taking.
Just like you willed yourself to be
taller than your dad,
you will be a success someday
in whatever you choose to do.

About Bob

It seems like yesterday that we first fell in love.
You were focused, driven, so sure of yourself
in your crisp white shirts, wild ties
and well-worn brown or black shoes,
the only shoes you owned.
Your straw blonde hair was neatly buzzed,
your passionate blue eyes
well hidden behind black rimmed glasses.
You don't look a lot different from those days
over thirty-five years ago
except for a few lines in your face,
and a waist that has grown an inch or two.
You still even have the buzz.

You are a true Renaissance man.
Though your forte is science and mathematics,
you can recite a Shakespearean sonnet
at the drop of a hat,
quote Goethe's couplets to a room
filled with a hundred engineers,
play guitar while belting out
Honky Tonk Woman or The House of the Rising Sun,
and spend your leisure time at
racket ball, golf, Sea Haven Towers,
Ultra Yatzee, solitaire,and your daily
and two Sunday crossword puzzles.
Nothing happens in the morning
until the crossword is done.

Those who know you will admit
you can be a tad impatient
especially behind the wheel.
You would rather drive through a maze of side streets
than wait for a traffic light.
Every chance you get you wield your lead foot
like a weapon of mass destruction.
ignoring my protests and cries of whiplash.
You'll just speed on,
pointing out other lawbreakers along the way.

You were a hard guy to reel in
but, once I did you were truly committed
to me, your sons and even your mother-in-law.
You fell in love with our boys from birth
never shying away from changing a diaper.
I can still picture you carrying them around on your back
telling them in your teacherly way
about the world around them
or going on and on at the dinner table
 about one subject or another
until they had to escape squealing,
"He's lecturing again."
And before you want to escape from this little lecture
here's one last thought.
Throughout the bumpy E ride of our years together
you have been my rock, my anchor, my strength.
You've worked hard for all your years.

The Secret to Fifty Years

We were married just over fifty years.
I was thirty and he thirty-three
So it was impossible to think we'd ever
Be married this long. In fact the odds
Were so against us, lasting more than
A year or two was a big surprise to some.
What was the glue that kept us together?
Well, for sure, our love for our sons
Paul and Ben. We also both worked
Outside our house most of those years,
sometimes even working side by side.
We also shared equally
In taking care of the boys and our house.
But the most important part
Was we gave each other space
To do our own things, whether pursuing a hobby
A political cause, a creative endeavor
Like today. I'm in my office writing
He's upstairs solving his daily puzzles
And we may not even see each other
Until we sit down to watch the news,
and have a glass of wine at six o'clock.

Have A Wonderful Day

Have a wonderful day
many have said in their
greetings to me
on my last birthday.
Some also ask what I'm going to do
on this special and auspicious day.
Those sentiments make me laugh.
What can I do when I can't
even go out to celebrate?
I took my usual big long walk,
had a bowl of cereal and berries
draped in oat milk for breakfast,
read the newspaper, read all the
Facebook birthday greetings,
and wrote thank yous for
all the new donations to
my birthday fundraiser, the
American Foundation for Suicide Prevention
to help stop the suicide epidemic
going on more so now because of
the coronavirus pandemic
and to honor my dead-by-suicide-son Paul.
So as of this morning
I've raised one thousand seven dollars.
That's a good day's fundraising work.
The rest of this day will go on as usual:
writing here for a while,
reading more of Karine Jean-Pierre's book,
Moving Forward: A Story of Hope,

Hard Work, and the Promise of America,
taking my late afternoon nap, which I need
to take right now, and having dinner.
One difference is we'll order food brought in
instead of my cooking.
Someone turning eighty needs
a good break from that on this
I-can't-believe-I've-lived-this-long
special day. Really do I only look sixty
as my son Ben says?
Nah! He's just being kind.

Writing Quality

Today is an upside-down day.
I walked early as usual
But decided to get
My grocery shopping out of the way
Before my shower and writing work.
Rather than the other way around.
So now I've got my ass in the chair
And fingers on my keyboard
After two-thirty in the afternoon.
The question is. Will the time
I write make a difference
In the quality of what I write?

Last Look

I spent over an hour today
plucking, shaving, showering,
shampooing, drying, ironing
my hair and lathering my face
and body with lotions
and ointments meant to keep me
moist and youthful.
I then put on clean clothes
carefully picked from all the items
unworn for months already.
When I take a last look in my mirror
I wonder what I did all that for.
I'm only going to come down
to my writing room, sit at my desk,
turn on my computer,
and write this poem. No need to do
any of that other stuff
to put these words on this page.

People Always Ask

How are you?
And I usually respond
I'm okay. Just okay?
They ask
And I say, Yes,
I can't get above okay.
That's how my life is.
It's lonely
It's pointless
It's void of a lot
Of people to love.
So it's just okay.
I have a nice
Place to live
I've made some friends
And I keep kind of busy
With writing and reading.
But right now
It's like I'm going
Around in circles
With no stopping point
No place to land
No one to hold me
And give me a comfortable
Place to carry on.

Business Day

This has been a day
To do business
At the bank
At the insurance companies.
And I even cancelled
Some services by email
And phone.
Plus a call came through
This afternoon.
The man asked if
Robert was there.
I bluntly said:
Robert is dead.
Don't call again.
It's about time
I take control
And let those sellers
Know who is in charge.
Just because I'm
An old woman
Doesn't mean I can't
Manage my money
And get someone
Off my back.

Well, Yes, Of Course

I'm not myself these days
How could I be?
In over three years
My whole life has changed.
My husband got deathly sick
And died.
I sold my house.
I either gave away, sold,
Or threw away at least
Half my things.
And here's what I'm left with:
A little apartment
In an old people's community,
Some pretty nice folks
I see once in a while,
Not so wonderful meals
And a few social activities.
The best thing I can do
For myself is take
My daily walk and
Listen to whatever podcast
Seems interesting
And then return here
And spend the
Rest of the day alone.

First Time

I was 25, divorced,
Working a good job
As a technical editor
Over in Redondo Beach –
A crazy commute
From my apartment, up in Bel Air.
But I liked them both
The job and the apartment.

I heard his voice
Over my cubicle wall.
He was talking to
My editor colleague
About the moon landing
and splash-down stuff,
you know, the lunar descent module,
Not anything my blue pencil
Had worked on yet.
Not anything I cared about right then either.

I wanted to have a look
At the guy with the voice
That kept talking, talking, talking.
I got up
Walked past the cubicle next-door
In my swinging knee-length skirt,
Clinging blouse buttoned up to my neck,
And 3-inch spiked heels,
With pointy bra,

Girdle and nylon stockings underneath
The kind of clothes girls had
To wear to work in those days
Until they let us wear slacks
A couple years later,
That had to be
Part of a suit.

When I walked by
I saw
A ruddy-faced lanky guy
With a blonde buzz
A brown suit,
White shirt and
A flowered tie
That didn't go so well
With the suit.
He looked up,
Sucking a pen between his lips.
And those big baby blues peering out
Behind his rimless specs
Hit me like OMG!

And all I could think about
Was how was I going to get to know that guy.
Later on, when we met
At his office in Washington DC –
That's a whole other story –
He told me
Yes, he felt the same OMG!
And you can guess what went on
From there.

Birds and Squirrels

Giant birds of paradise grow
in my yard
so tall I can see them
outside our third-floor window.
This year those huge flowers
are clumped together like
an AA group grope.
Dark blue pointy nests
cradle white winged petals
right where the banana leaves
spread out from their stem.
Now I've waited long and hard
for these blooms,
probably over twenty years.
And when I saw that damn squirrel
nestle its nose right into the clump
I wished I had a shot gun
to pop it off.
Not only did it nestle
it sat there pulling out the white sepals
the dark blue pointy bract
was supposed to protect,
like that damn rodent was taunting me.
I could see it giving me the eye
as it dropped those white petals
one by one
to the gravel path below.
I yelled at that intrusive squirrel
again and again.

It ran away again and again.
But, that little twerp kept coming back,
nestling in so deep,
so furiously, as if it were in bird paradise,
the plant shook from its core.
I don't know if birds
with dark blue and white flowers are poisonous,
but a few days later
we found a squirrel corpse
on the ground
next to its white petal prey.
Would you say it got what it deserved?
maybe, maybe not.
Yes, what the heck,
I would.

New York Impressions

A couple of weeks ago
I walked around New York City
in the heat and humidity
amidst the filth, trash
and black globs of gum
ground flat on the sidewalks.

The crowds were so thick.
I needed turn signals to turn left on foot
or to get the right of way when crossing the streets.
The hordes kept walking into me
without even a glance or concern.
Girls of all sizes wore shorts
rolled up so high
their asses hung out.

People in red-shirts hustled city tours, Ripley tours,
Hudson River boat tours, and Madame Tussaud's.
Everywhere I looked I saw them in all shapes and sizes
and heard every language imaginable.
Some didn't walk.
The homeless sat on the sidewalks
up against buildings,
their heads hanging,
with a begging sign in front of them.
Others dressed like comic book characters
begging tourists to pose with them.
You should have seen the tall guy

in only his cowboy boots
and skimpy speedos
and the beauties he recruited.
Even hailing a taxi escape didn't work.
Taxis crawled amidst trucks, busses,
emergency vehicles, and Ubers
But I'm sure their meters didn't care.
Finally, I stopped for a drink
at the hundred-year-old Plaza Hotel
on the corner of Fifth and Central Park West
and needled the aloof waiter to break a smile
for a bit of comic relief.

No

I don't know why I say yes
when I should be saying no.
This time I said yes
to a consulting job to edit a document
at the aerospace company
I used to work for.
There I sit, three days a week,
in a freezing windowless room
huddled in an old sweater and wool socks,
my eyes glued to the computer screen
without a breather for hours at a time.
My right index finger scrolls the mouse
while I add or subtract a word or two
to the written text, reorganize the outline,
turn capitalized words into all lower case,
and define acronyms.
It makes my eyes tear, my fingers numb,
my back ache, my ankles swell, and for what?
A pittance, a few extra bucks
that I could very well do without.

Instead I could be with my muse
at my desk at home
Looking out to the trickling fountain in my yard,
writing Charles Bukowski–like poems
or doing what I need to be doing the most,
writing my own book,
Next time, my answer will be
not just no, but a NO in all caps.

Like One

They sit turned toward each other
on the sofa.
She a slim woman,
her hair long and blonde.
He tall and buff,
his hair thinning in spots.
Both their faces show
lines, dark circles.
Yes, they've weathered a few storms.
Gazing in each other's eyes,
hers deep blue rimmed in black lashes
his hazel with crinkles in the corners.
They squeeze and entwine their fingers,
sip red wine,
savoring the smooth berry flavors
trickling down their throats,
then take a last bite
of her chocolate fondant.
She leans over,
wipes away a tear
from the side of his cheek.
He brushes a bit
of fondant from her chin.
They rise,
still holding tight
they start to dance
so slow they barely move.
His hand firm on her back,
her face nestled into his shoulder.
He turns out the lights,

slips her gray silk dress
off her shoulders and over her hips
into a heap on the floor
and leads her to bed.
He strips, moves on top of her.
They explore, taste
and feel every inch, every pore,
stroking faces, necks, thighs, feet,
kissing mouths open,
almost swallowing each other.
Kissing their tongues reaching
down their throats.
Coupling, coming,
one on top, then the other.
Spooned, joined
until they rest
so close they are like one
under the crumpled sheets.

Poem Hunting at the Coffee Bean

Amidst the jarring noises of scrapping chairs,
rattling utensils, and blending machines,
a poem walks by with long legs
in shorts rolled up so high
her ass hangs out.
Her skimpy top is pink,
so is her computer,
trimmed with shiny stars
and butterflies. The next minute
she's outside on her phone
pacing up and back,
frowning slightly, pulling her blond hair
out of her ponytail clip.

Another poem sits across from me
tapping into his smart phone
with lips pursed. I wonder
if he's distressed or it's his normal façade.
He looks casual in flip flops and flying shirt tails,
but, really, his red sweaty face says it all.

I turn to a young girl
in a sheer turquoise shirt.
She points her boobs at
the tall boy across from her
as they do their schoolwork.
While talking more than studying,
she chomps on her gum,

probably not so good
for the braces on her teeth.

Another couple on my left, sit side by side.
She looks intently onto her computer screen.
He, with his arm around her, strokes her
shoulder – his free hand resting right
under her shirt sleeve. Hmm.
Cozy homework at the Coffee Bean.

And then I see long legs leave
on the back of her boyfriend's motorcycle.
He set a pink helmet over her blonde hair,
before he revved off.

Eclipse – The Path to Totality

We planned for months
to travel to Oregon
to see a total eclipse
of the sun – the first time visible
coast to coast in the US since 1918.

My sister picked a gorgeous garden,
the Oregon Garden,
in Silverton for our viewing.
She also invited friends
and our nephew from Seattle and his family.

Before we left LA
people warned the crowds would be horrendous,
the traffic bumper to bumper for miles,
and it gave me pause.
Should we still go on this trip
to see a once in a lifetime
occurrence that would last
less than two minutes?
Of course, we went.
My husband, an amateur astronomer,
would have it no other way.
And we were not disappointed.

We left Portland in the dark of the morning
of Monday, August 21,
at five am to be exact,
and it took us all of fifty minutes

to get to our garden destination.
What happened to the predicted traffic?
Lines of cars inching along the highways,
never materialized.
When we arrived
it was just getting light
and still cold.

We found our viewing area
amongst native yellow, purple, and red blooms
and hordes of bees and yellow jackets
vying with us for a place on this ground.
But we prevailed.
All eleven of us set up
our low-backed folding chairs,
ate a light poorly cooked breakfast,
drank our $3.00 bottles of water,
got out our special glasses,
and snuggled in to wait.

At nine-oh-five
the moon took its first tiny bite
out of the sun's upper right corner
and the event we came to see
was on its way.
After a few minutes
more of the sun disappeared.
As the moon passed in front of the sun
it created a large yellow crescent first
that got smaller and smaller and smaller still
until it looked like a sliver –
all the while turning the temperature down,
darkening the sky and

quieting the buzzing bees.
At precisely ten eighteen
yells and cheers erupted throughout the garden.
The moon had completely blocked the sun,
leaving a black hole surrounded
by a brilliant corona and a diamond ring
so spectacular, you had to be there.

The children in our family, ages eleven and twelve,
watched with the rest of us.
Cool, they said, agreeing that this was
an experience they'd never forget.

Number 933

They tore down the old house
Where I grew up
It was brown brick
With a huge front lawn
Where we raked leaves every fall
Into big bundles for burning
On the street
Where we shoveled snow
Off the long narrow driveway
In the cold, cold winter,
From where I biked a mile to and from
School four times a day.
We moved away when I was nineteen
And I would drive by
Every once in a while
When I was in town.
But not anymore.
I don't want to see the replacement house
They built to erase
The trials, the dreams, the hopes
I had living at number 933
During my girlhood days.

The Stoop

After he left for work,
dressed in his khakis, white shirt
his brown book bag slung
across his body,
I would see him sometimes
sitting on the stoop
outside of Starbucks
drinking his coffee
smoking his cigarette
leaning over with his head down.
I wondered what he thought sitting there.
Was he already planning his death?
Or was he thinking about his beloved
who lived on the other coast.
It seemed their love was doomed.
She wanted him to be whole, but
he wouldn't take his meds and comply.
I worried each time they met
would be their last.
He is gone now
She's married and a mother of two
and I see other thoughtful young men
on that stoop every time I pass
hoping their fate
will not be the same
as my boy's.

My Big Kitchen Aid

I brought it a new cover
from our time in Sicily –
a colorful dish towel,
white, trimmed with red
and little pictures
of Sicily's important cities
covering its background.
I tucked the towel snugly
around its big stainless-steel bowl
and up and around
the stand that firmly
holds its mixers.
I've had this mixer
for forty years at least
and used it quite a bit at first –
for whipping cream while slowly adding
powdered sugar just the way
my husband likes it,
for mixing all the ingredients
for cheesecake way back when
I could still eat dairy,
and for kneading dough using
its special dough hook
during my bread baking days.
Now, the poor old mixer –
and, of course, I had to have
the most expensive one –
stands unused on my kitchen counter
wrapped up neatly
in a pretty towel.

Covered Mirrors

As one addicted to looking at myself
In the mirror, I often wonder
What it would be like
To have none in my house.
Even my husband asks
Why I should be still concerned
With how I look at my age.
I have no answer to that.
Instead I go back
To whatever I do
In front of the mirror –
Putting on makeup, plucking my eyebrows,
Styling my hair, parading in front of it
in my outfit of the day.

The only respite I get from those pesky mirrors
Is visiting the bereaved after a loved one's death
The Jewish law says
we must not worship an image
Or stand in front of one – like a picture or mirror –
In a house of worship.
So we cover all mirrors
In the house of the bereaved,
A temporary house of worship,
During Shiva, the seven-day mourning period.
It's a good way to avoid self-adoration
And being overly concerned with my own image.
Covering the mirrors helps us
Concentrate on mourning
The death of our loved ones.

True Love

Everyday he says
I love you
He looks through
His blue eyes
Leans in close
To tell me
He loves me
More than ever
Every passing year
I smile sigh
And also say
I love you
It's like a
Promise and gift
That we'll still
Love each other
For another many, many
Years, at least!

Sheer Hate!

I can't stand him
I really can't stand him.
And I have to see him every damn day
as he struts slowly around the gym
hardly exercising.
Instead he chats
or uses the weight machines
as easy chairs
where he sits and drinks coffee.

That's not why I hate him
and will never ever
look him in the eye
or speak to him.

Years ago our small sons were pals.
They played on the same soccer team
that this man coached.
He'd strut up and down the field then too,
one hand in his pocket,
the other emphasizing the directions
he yelled so loud
he even scared me.
He yelled at my son too
and benched him so much
my boy never played soccer again.

Tricks with Numbers

The number eighty-three
Is not a trick
It's a fact that says
I've gotten old,
I don't have long
In this world
I have lived most of my life already.
And I don't mind.
I've lived a full life
Full of good, full of bad
And surpassed the seventy-two years
My grandfather, grandmother, father
And brother had.
Only my mother lived longer
All the way to ninety-four
But she was such a miserable woman
As she approached her end
We all couldn't wait
To see her go.
Now, why would I want
To live that long
And become such a nuisance
That people would be glad
To see me
Buried in the ground?

My Dad's Gold Watch

He didn't get it for
Excellent service at some company
No. This son of a shoemaker
Bought the watch himself
In the mid 1940s to celebrate
His own success
And he wore it proudly every day
For the rest of his life.
In a gold setting, its large round white face
With gold roman numerals told the time.
Its wide woven gold band
Snapped together around his left wrist.
The watch fit him fine at first,
But as he aged the band fit looser
And looser, like a clunky bracelet.
After my dad died my brother
Got the watch.
But never wore it once.
It was too gold for him, I guess.
That's why I'm wearing it now.

Romeo and Juliet's Wedding Night

The black drapes open
and on center stage is a bed
covered in heavy red quilts and pillows
with a red satin cloth sweeping up
into the rafters from the headboard.
The bed covers and white sheets crumple in heaps
by the bodies of the two lovers on the top,
then underneath,
then on the pillows at the foot of the bed,
then on the floor
as they wrap their arms and legs around each other,
first one on top and then the other,
never separating as they kiss and hug and stroke each other
until almost daylight and it is time to part.
But still they don't part.
While he pulls up his trousers, buttons his shirt, tucking it in
halfway,
she, wrapped in a sheet,
her long dark hair covering her breasts like a halter,
her arms out to him,
kneels on the bed,
pleading, "Don't go, not yet,"
calling to him to come back
crying in full soprano voice,
"It's not light yet."
And he turns around and looks into her eyes.
His tenor voice roars,
"Yes, I'll stay,"
and he tears off his clothes again

leaps back onto the bed again
pushes her back down
and enfolds her in his arms — again.

At daybreak, finally getting up,
picking his clothes off the floor,
he dresses, this time for good.
He pulls her to him,
crushes her body against his
and jumps over the balcony
to the ladder.
He begins to climb down and stops,
looks back up at her on the bed,
the new light glow on her pale face.
He raises one hand to her.
She runs out to the railing,
Leaning, reaching, stretching her arms out to him,
until she almost falls over,
Their fingers touch once more
before he climbs down and runs from her,
before the full morning light discovers them together
on this their wedding night.
And, we all know,
but don't want to know
that this was their last night together
alive.

Sixty-two

It meant I could get into most movie theaters
On a senior ticket, and, if I chose,
Begin to collect social security.
But, that was for those old folks over there
I was too young for that senior stuff.
I could still do more crunches than most 30-year olds
And walk a 15-minute mile. I was fit and trim
And my doctor said, disgustingly healthy.
So, what do I care if I'm age 62?
My age has nothing to do with me.

Writer's Block

I'm dried out. I can't find the right words today
Like other times when they flow so freely my pen
Can't catch up. I don't understand how on some days
I have more to say than time to write it all down
While on others like today I stumble over every syllable,
I search my brain for exactly the right word.
But, it isn't the job of the artist to give up
I must continue to squeeze out the last drops of my thoughts
Onto the page like a toothpaste tube
Delivering its last trickle of paste to the brush.

Giggling Girls

I feel deserted. They all left me this afternoon
Bob to play golf, Ben to hunt for an apartment
Even the workmen left after less than half a day.
But, I'm not lonely. I like the solitude of my writing life.
Now, I can sit in this almost deserted bakery,
Sipping a glass of tea and listen to two teenage girls
Giggling in the booth beside me. I don't mind them
Their youth, their looks, their flowing hair carelessly pinned back,
Their slinky tight, low-riding jeans that let their navels show.
Oh, I was born much too early.
I would have loved to wear today's outfits.
But, no, I was a teenager in the 50s,
Wearing prim dresses with peter pan collars,
Full skirts that fell way below my knees
Pulled together with a narrow belt at the waist.
Even so, I found lots to giggle about then too.

Another View of New York

New York City
Union Square, the lower East side
Paul's country.
He blossomed there
He became a musician there
While he learned about
Cold fourth floor walkups,
Dealers hustling on street corners
Late night gigs, playing for tips in smoky bars
Fast walking just to keep warm
And a first grownup love affair.

I went back there last month.
No, he wasn't there.
He's been dead and gone many years now
But the reminders were everywhere.

The square where he first lived as
A freshman at the New School
In the tall skinny brick building
66 Park Avenue where the Jazz Department
Held classes and had practice rooms and jam sessions
And young musicians aspiring for fame.
It was on the marble steps of that building
Where he and the girl
With the long flowing auburn hair and piercing blue eyes
Became the love of his life.
No, she was his life.

Driving the Cote d'Azur

I drove that little red car
Along the Azur coast
Where the sea was like lapis blue
Deep, cold and choppy from
The wind ripping around us.
It was a treacherous drive
Cars on all sides
People walking the boardwalk
Or crossing the road
Not heeding the traffic as they
Went where and as they pleased
And I working the pedals
The clutch almost exclusively
Still unused to its feel.
My first car was a stick shift
Almost 50 years ago.
Interesting how old skills don't die
But can surface up
From the dregs of memory in faraway places
And at unexpected times.

Watching Tennis in August

The sexy, buff girls of tennis came every August
To play their game in Manhattan Beach
Champions all of them
They loved the crowds
They thrived on the electricity, the adoration of their fans
The shouts:
We love you Monica, Come on, Martina,
You can do it Serena, Lindsey
The groans over a ball slammed into the net
The oohs and ahs during a long rally
The cheers when a winning ball skimmed the line.

They all had their own style
Number 1, Martina Hingis,
Named for the great Navratilova,
Looked delicate, graceful and aloof out there,
Always with a wide, toothy smile
Hair smoothed back just so
Had a shrewd strategy
That out lasted most of her opponents

Now sleek sans 30 pounds,
Lindsey Davenport, the nice girl on the tour
Looking tall and gangly and awkward
Fooled us with her
Killer serve, hard, fast, flat
Ground strokes and a bullet volley
That almost no one could return

Monica Seles, the come back kid.
Was the ultimate professional
So poised, so focused with her eyes
Always on her racket
Fingers plucking at the strings
Until time to make one of her perfect angle shots
No opponent could reach

And the youngster of the greats,
Serena Williams, still making a fashion statement
With her long Rodman style braids,
Wild-colored dresses with shoes to match
Sashayed confidently around the court,
Wiggling her ass and jiggling her boobs
As she got ready for the next point
But she was not all show
She knew how to really rip those balls across the net
Leaving her opponents swishing their rackets at the air.

I sat there for one week
Every year in August
In my second-row box seat.
Eyes glued to the stadium court
Sweltering under the sun during the day
Slathered in sun block and wearing
My wide-brimmed straw hat
While shivering beneath my lap robe during
Night play under the lights
I revelled in the circus, this happening scene
Taking such joy as these young, beautiful, toned,
Athletic girls in their clingy short skirts, tight tops
And designer jewelry
Hit the hell out of that fuzzy little yellow ball.

Many Beds

Tomorrow by this time
I'll be home in my own bed
That's where I want to be the most.
Not that our many beds
These last few weeks
Have not been wonderful.
Just think about it:
Falmouth just across the bay
From Martha's Vineyard
Boston in a lovely suite with Ben in the
Living room
Our first hotel in Paris – funky and seedy
But still friendly
Toulouse on the capital square in
The Grand Hotel de l'Opera.
Then on to St. Remy en Provence – A lovely hostelry
Just outside of town complete
With swimming pool, golf course and fitness room.
Another move to four days at St. Jean Cap Ferrate
At the elegant Le Voile D'Or where we
Ate breakfast each morning
Looking at the Mediterranean Sea.
Rochegude was next
A 12th Century castle
Where I felt like I could master the world, but
Only for a few short minutes.
After a drive in the pounding rain
We reached beautiful Annecy and
L'Auberge de Pere Bise – sometimes haughty

Always accommodating
And the most beautiful place of all.
Next to last – the lovely Lyon Vieux
Lyon's old town and La tour Rose
I felt so fortunate to be there.
And finally here, back in Paris
On the Left Bank near St. Germaine des Pres
The Lutetia – they can keep it
It only makes me long for my own bed
All the more.

The Couple at the Gym

(in three acts)

Act One
He reminds me of a Svengali
as he waits for her at the bench.
In his baseball hat and long sweats,
his backpack slung over one shoulder,
he paces, looks around, adjusts his workout gloves
until she appears.
She arrives, her black hair
done up in a pony tail,
she has a movie star's face,
and a body without a pinch of fat.
He leads, she follows him into the gym
and they workout side by side
on equipment of his choosing.
He hands her the weights,
she complies with the dictated reps.
He finds two treadmills for their next set
and she like the good girl
jumps on one of them and performs.
They don't talk except when he orders her
to pick up her speed.
He's too occupied singing along with the music
flowing through his ear buds.
She just works out, looking pretty.
And so it goes.
Svengali and the good girl.

I see them everyday
at the gym.

Act Two
The beautiful girl
with the thick black hair
and pale skin
came back to the gym this week.
She hardly looks like she
just had a baby.
Her waist is tiny
her breasts don't show
a hint of droop,
and the rest of her body
is toned and trim.
She is the Hedy Lamar type
always perfectly made up
to show off her
deep black eyes and
full red mouth
even while working out.
It's all so unnecessary.
She'd turn anyone's head
without even a drop of makeup.
That's how striking this beauty is.

Act Three
The girl with dark hair and eyes,
you know the one I mean,
now has a name.
She is Donna.
And I found out she's
of part Persian descent.

Well that accounts for her beauty.
And the Asian guy
who barks workout instructions
like a sergeant
is not her husband.
Whew! I was glad to hear that!
And, no she's not a Hollywood star
though those moguls could
use her looks over there.
I'm told she's a lawyer,
just sworn into the bar a day or two
before she had her baby son.
And even though she doesn't wear a ring
at least not to the gym
she has a Persian husband.
What a lucky guy.
This is a girl who takes good care of herself
and she's probably just as good to him.

Preparing to Go

Even on the elliptical machine this morning,
reading my New Yorker
about the faux Rockefeller, Clark,
I kept thinking: should I add a couple
more shirts? Should I pick out some
silver jewelry? Do I need a pair of dressy heels?
Even while Jeffery complimented my Pilates form,
I kept seeing the piles on the sofa:
shirts, pants, undies, jackets, hats, and scarves,
shoes scattered on the floor, and the stuff bought
especially for safari in Kenya and Tanzania:
a camera with built in telescopic lens,
insect repellent, and a bite-itch eraser.
I couldn't stop asking myself
what could I add or take away?
Even while I did my last Yoga stretches,
I churned about what else I had to do:
gather up my toiletries
and put them in travel containers,
pack my contact lens solutions and case,
lay out clothes for traveling tomorrow.
At least I had distributed
my vitamins into separate baggies.
At least I picked everything up at the cleaner
and finished the last load of laundry.
Yet still weighing on my mind was
how much everything weighed.
Would my soft duffle be allowed
on those teeny African two-engine planes
if over the imposed thirty-three pound limit?

Ode to Stanley

I really didn't know you well.
Once in a while you stayed out
on the curbside of my home
or you picked me up
so Ben and I could go to lunch.
I never thought much about you.
You were small and gray –
a rather drab gray at that.
Then one night you showed your true stuff,
that you were not that drab after all –
even when you were hit
three times on the freeway
pushed across one lane to the next,
still sleek from the recent rainstorm,
until you finally stopped in the fast lane
facing the oncoming traffic.
With your front end falling off
and dents all over, you proved your worth.
You sacrificed your life for your driver's.
That's what I call valor, living up
to your safety first reputation.
You saved my son's life – you
saved all our lives.
And after all that
they'll just smash you into a little cube.
Well, perhaps you'll get recycled
into an even better automobile.
Yes, definitely you should be reincarnated.
And if you are, maybe I'll be lucky
to have you as my own.

Still Life

I walk up behind her.
Her champagne-colored skirt
billows up showing
her matching panties,
and long straight legs
spread wide.
I walk around
to see her face on
and find a Marilyn
smiling, happy,
her red lips parted,
eyes closed.
She holds her skirt
to keep the wind
from flying it up in front
as a pleated halter
in the same champagne color
keeps her breasts
exactly in the right place.
This Marilyn,
strong, substantial,
built larger than life,
belies the insecure,
melancholy Marilyn
who left us
over fifty years ago.

Sock Hop

The three girls took turns
at the dressing table
tinkering with their hair,
polishing their nails and applying
mascara, rouge, and lipstick
to their clear and smooth
school girl complexions.
They took their time
donning their full skirts,
so they puffed out just right
over oodles of petticoats.
They squeezed into tight fuzzy sweaters,
accessorized perfectly with
belts, collars, necklaces, and barrettes.
When they finished they
twirled one by one
in front of the mirror.
Diane's hair gleamed
as it flowed down her back
and just over one eye.
Her pale pink sweater,
adorned with a single strand of pearls,
and a wide patent leather belt.
Vicky was a vision in all black –
her sweater, her skirt, her shoes,
and her trademark headband
used to tame her unruly hair.
Only her bobby sox, her belt,
and the little pique peter pan collar

contrasted in white.
She gave her skirt a few pats
and was raring to go.
Betty, the little pixie, looked adorable.
The pin curls she
wound just around her face
gave her short hair a soft, feminine look.
Her full navy skirt
and fuzzy white angora sweater fit her to a T.
Finally ready, they jumped into Betty's
Chevy turquoise and white convertible
and drove away
hoping for invitations to slow dance
from the boys of their dreams.

Even A Broken Foot

Accidents are just that —accidents.
Yet some can be avoided
like my husband's the other night.
He walked willy-nilly toward a dark room
that the hotel should have had well lit.
And while groping in the dark
for a light switch
he fell down a short flight of stairs,
rewarded with immediate pain
in his foot and ankle.
Perhaps a quick application of ice
gave us false hope that it would take
no further care but
elevation and an Ace bandage.
But more swelling, more pain
indicated x-rays were in order.
The prognosis, a broken foot
not to be walked upon for four to six weeks
Now enclosed in a cast
and crutches prescribed for mobility
there's whining and demands already.
So I wonder
where it says in the marriage vows
for better or worse
and a broken foot?

How Old Are You?

Golda Meir asked,
"How old would you be
if you didn't know your age?"

In my mind
I'd still be a young girl of 25 or 30,
not anywhere near 70.
I feel young and vital and productive.
I work full time
I work out every day
And I still have a young person's dreams
of climbing down the Grand Canyon
running a marathon
playing competitive tennis
and writing my first novel.
I have most of the world to see –
India, Australia, Israel
and northern Europe.
And I dream of living
for a time in my beloved Italy.
In fact, I have to stop myself
from setting goals I should have made
forty years ago
I like to think I have all the time in the world
I feel that young.
Only my husband reminds me
I do not.
And he's right.
So, I've decided I better get started.

I've got a lot to do with whatever time
I have left now that
my chronological age
says I'm old.

Sleepless

I lay there in one spot
my cheek on just a corner
of my pillow.
My body drawn up
in a fetal ball,
one hand on the side
of my butt
the other on its
opposite shoulder.
And for the longest time
I counted:
one, two, three, four, five
over and over again.
I could feel the drifting come
and then something would interrupt it
Bob getting up
my nose being squished
my neck stiff and hurting.
And then I'd drift and count again
until the next I knew
I heard the classical music play
in the background of my dream
of a lovely ride on the train.

The Long Farewell

Let's have a long farewell
like young lovers used to do
at the train station.
She, in a flowing white dress
with gloves, shoes, and hat to match.
He in his new gray suit,
shiny wingtips,
and perfect bow tie
bends her backward
in an embrace
that makes people gape
as they go by.
When they finally come up for air
he takes her face in his hands
kisses both her cheeks
and gives her another big hug.
She can't help responding.
She entwines her arms
around his neck
and snuggles her face
into his chest.
But, she must leave him
and teary eyed
she turns to go to the train.
No. He's not ready to let her go.
He takes her hands
then, as she backs away,
they staying in touch

just by the fingertips
until they can reach each other no longer.
As she steps onto train
she blows him kisses.
He takes his handkerchief
from his suit pocket
and begins to wave
and he keeps waving,
all the while saying
farewell, farewell,
until she is out of sight.

Porsche Wine

Wine pourers in Amador County
like to say
this is a nice porch wine.
Not to be confused with wines
drunk with a meal,
porch wines are to be sipped
while watching the sunset
or the ocean or the people going by
on your porch or veranda or
deck or patio or stoop
or whatever you like to call
an outside area at your home
where you can just sit
and enjoy life's little pleasures.
One of our winery hosts
tells the story of a visitor
who had a bit of a hearing problem,
who misunderstood the word
porch for Porsche.
Now it would be nice to have a wine
just for sipping in a Porsche
but when would one do it?
Certainly not for driving –
that would be against the law,
and certainly not while parked in front of your porch.
Porsche's aren't the kind of vehicle
one leaves immobile very long –
even if the wine is so good
it makes everything
stop in its tracks.

White Picket Fence

Don't you remember
I could hardly wait to leave?
All I needed was my new red VW to arrive
from Germany –
I called it Lady Bug –
and then I packed up
the 800 square-foot house
we rented in West Los Angeles
in one weekend flat.

Don't you remember
that I left all the stuff belonging to your family?
the crystal art deco vase,
your precious kitchen utensils,
and the baby grand piano,
even though no one played it but me.

Don't you remember
you ignored me
as I lay in the hospital for
three days when our baby miscarried?
You never visited once.
All you said on the drive to the hospital was,
"Shove a pillow between your legs."
You didn't want the blood pouring out of me
to ruin the upholstery of your car.

How could you blame me
for having my first affair

with the six foot four Greek DJ
we met that New Year's Eve?
His mellow voice on the radio spoke only to me.
I couldn't resist combing my fingers
through his dark hair
and smoothing his pale cheeks with my thumbs.
I had to climb up on a chair
to reach his face when we kissed.
No matter that he turned out to be
a bigger shit than you,
at least he knew about romance.
He gave me the courage to leave.

Did you really think I'd be moved
when you called the other day
from the Indian reservation in Bishop CA
where you live with your fifth wife.
And told me
that you've been sober for fifteen years,
newly diagnosed with bipolar disorder,
and that you still long
for that house with a white picket fence
where the two of us, still married,
could have lived out our days?

No, sir that would never have happened.
I'm the one who left you.

But I'd be glad to offer you a lemonade
if you want to visit – only because
I'm curious to see what
your once handsome Marlon Brando-looks
turned into after fifty years.

Portrait Poem

He sits at the table
head leaning to the side
eyes closed
mouth open just a bit.
His cheeks are ruddy
From fever or infection
Or from leaning them
On his hands.
His blue shirt and sweater
Almost match.
He looks cozy over there
As he breathes easily
Softly. Yet every once
In a while he lets out
A hacking cough,
Setting off my worries
My dark fantasies about
The possibility of losing
him at any time.

Case History

His medical case history
these past few weeks scares me.
First it's a rasping cough
that lasts so long
it turns into a month-long pneumonia.
Once he feels better
he goes on ever increasing length walks
and even works out
at the gym for a half hour.
He sees the doctor
who prescribes
antibiotics and an increase
in his Lasix consumption to get rid
of the extra fluid in his body.
He's finally showing signs of recovery.
But I won't get my hopes up
until his ills are finally cured.
Only then can I give
my caregiving chores
a final rest.

My Fave Is Avocado

I don't much care about food
I eat to live, you might say.
And I'm a creature of habit.
I'll eat the same things day after day
like my usual peanut butter
and blueberries breakfast.
But I do have a favorite –
I love avocados.
No matter how much fat they have
no matter how bland they taste
I must have some avocado,
whether plain or in a salad
most every day.
Yesterday I was offered avocado sushi
at our local Japanese restaurant
and I couldn't resist.
There appeared three perfect avocado slices
attached to sushi rice with a strip of seaweed
on a small plate,
and after a little dip in some soy sauce
I took a bite. It was perfect.
Yes, I'll be going back for more.

Moving to Catch Up

I begin my day
In the heat of actions.
I get up,
turn off the alarm clock
Do my bathroom ablutions
Weigh myself
Change into gym clothes
Take my early morning medications,
Gulp down my first glass of water,
Get in my car
Drive myself to the gym
Walk to the front door
From the farthest parking spot
Check in
Fill my water bottle
And if I'm lucky
Grab my favorite elliptical machine
Set the timer,
Turn on my music
Open my New Yorker
And workout for ninety minutes.
After that, it's all downhill.
Now I'm at my least active state
Sitting at my desk
Moving my fingers on the keyboard
Working on an action poem.

Platinum

Chemical element with symbol **Pt**
And atomic element number 78,
My favorite metal,
Platinum, is primordial,
Which means it has existed in its current form,
Since before the earth was born.
It is transition metal and solid
With a noble stature.
Platinum has remarkable resistance
To corrosion
A good thing for holding
Precious stones in its hands.
For it is precious itself,
Gray-white in color
It is dense, malleable, ductile
And highly unreactive,
Making it the metal jeweler's
Prefer to work with. I know my stones
Look their best set in platinum,
And it keeps them perfectly safe.

Too Old to Travel?

I don't like to travel much anymore
Even for a weekend.
The packing,
The luggage lugging
The strange bed
And being always at the mercy
Of rich and salty restaurant food
Are beyond my tolerance level.
I'm getting too old
And tired to travel
Like I did in the past
Even fulfilling all the
Trips still on my bucket list –
Israel, Australia and New Zealand,
And living a month or two
In Rome
May be more than I can do.
Maybe if I take it slowly,
Allow more time at home
In between, I'll be able to
Still venture out.
But pretty soon I'll be too old
To do even that.

Number One on My Bucket List

My Bucket List was mentioned
In my first blog post
Way back in 2007.
Yet it took me ten years
To complete Item One
To climb down and back up
The Grand Canyon.
Finally a younger couple agreed
To go with us and made reservations
A year in advance.
The two women would go by foot
The men on mules.
That was the mistake.
My husband was badly injured
By the mule's saddle horn
And had to be med-evacuated
Out of there.
Unbeknown to us, we women
Kept climbing down
A terrain of rocky boulders, sand,
And constant hairpin turns,
Causing me to fall four times.
And there was no other way out
The next day but to climb back up.
Although this was always going to be
A one-time event,
I learned another huge lesson
Don't even attempt it one-time
At ages 76 and 80 respectively.
My husband and I are both lucky.

The Salad

Before I considered the enormity of it
I volunteered to bring the salad
As my contribution to our friend's dinner party
For ten.
I make salads all the time,
So I thought how hard could it be
To make a salad for an Indian themed dinner.
All I'd have to do is Google Indian salads
And I would be all set.
Well, not so fast.
There was a huge array of Indian salads
Over there at Google, way too many
To look at everyone.
Finally sometime in the middle
Of the week before the party,
I settled on one. It looked like
It had the right flavors: lime, cumin, mint, cilantro,
Serrano chili
And the right ingredients: cucumber, tomatoes,
Red onion, radishes.
But I decided it was missing two important
Things: oil for the lime dressing and lettuce.
I decided to take away the recipe's call for a chopped apple
And add in olive oil and bib lettuce,
That way the dish would be a little more conventional.
So, when party day came around
I shopped and found the reddest tomatoes in the store,
The Persian cucumbers I had never heard of
And the rest of my goods for a mere $50.

I began cooking two hours before
It was time to get dressed and leave for dinner
And believe me it took all that time:
Squeezing limes, chopping cilantro and mint, cutting cucumbers,
Tomatoes, radishes, and onions into tiny pieces,
And then adding the seasonings.
I mixed all those ingredients together, then washed and tore the
lettuce,
Intending to mix it in later with the dressing.
Speaking of, the dressing was another matter.
I found a lime dressing also at Google,
But it was only for a small supply.
I needed dressing for ten salads, so I made a cup of lime
And added a cup of oil plus loads of salt and pepper.
That turned out to be a little overkill, but the mixture worked.
The salad that I worried over for days also worked.
It got rave reviews. My husband who hardly ever
Eats salad liked it so much he asked me to make it again for him.
That's a big ask. Spending two hours on a salad
Would really be a labor of love. I'm not so sure
I'm up to it yet.

Making Room for Me

After six years I stacked Paul's books and records,
once in alphabetical order on his closet shelves,
in boxes out in the garage,
and finally cleared away all the dust.

I recreated his room and closet,
with a new hardwood floor,
a bay picture window, deep taupe walls,
a white ceiling and crown molding,
and file drawers and book shelves
for storing my poems.

After six years I recreated his room into a place
where I could finish telling his story and mine,
about his bipolar illness
and how the medicines didn't work for him,
about how hard he fought against taking his meds
because he couldn't live with them
and he couldn't live without them,
about his suicide
and how I survive through it all.

I am writing this story in his room.
I write sitting at a draftsman table opposite the bay window.
When I sit there
I sometimes gaze out to the garden,
at the three palm trees,
the small cement pond
where birds take a dip,

the ginger and azalea plants and my smiling Buddha.
I can hear the gurgle of the fountain
when it's warm enough
to leave the window open.

I feel a calm in his room
that helps my writing.
Maybe my reminders of Paul also help,
his candlesticks on the top shelf
of the bookcase,
his photo and a charcoal and white chalk drawing
of me when I was pregnant with him,
and a photo of a sunset taken on September 22, 1999,
his last night alive,
showing an orange sun
floating into the sea.
I also have an assemblage
of felt-covered wooden mallets
once used to strike the strings of a piano –
the instrument that kicked off his music career
when he was 10 years old.

No, I haven't erased him.
He is in there with me.
He is inside me.
Always.

Seventy Years Ago

Just after stepping off the train
I went into the phone booth with my mother.
She had to call her mother to tell her we came home
safe and sound.
She always called her mother.
She called her everyday.
My mother laid the newspaper
down by the phone, and while she talked
I could see the front-page picture.
It covered the whole page.
A picture of the girl, Suzanne,
who had been murdered.
When my mother got off the phone
she tried to hide it from me.
But I already saw it and knew
they had just found her head.
Pretty soon the whole story came pouring out
as my father drove us home from the station.
He and my mother talked while
my brother and I listened in the back seat.
The girl was taken from her second floor bedroom,
and I got scared. My bedroom was on the second floor.
The murderer climbed up there with a ladder
he found in the yard.
He climbed into her bedroom while she was asleep
and took her away, killed her,
and chopped her up.
And this morning, just before we got home
from our winter vacation trip

they found her head.
But they hadn't found the person who killed her yet.
They also found her ear in my school playground.
At least that's what the boy down the street said.
He also told me Suzanne lived three blocks
from us, on the second floor,
her bedroom facing the yard, just like mine.
And that she was our same age – five years old.
After that happened, I had to have the light on
in my room when I went to bed.
Every night, I crawled way down under the covers
so my head wouldn't stick out.
So he couldn't see me sleeping there
if he climbed up a ladder
to take me away too.

The Landscape

We visit our son in his grave
On his death day and birthday
Every year. Entering the iron gates
We wind around
To the cemetery's back section
The place they bury cremated remains.
He's under a small marble headstone
Simply worded beloved son and brother
With a tiny chiseled piano nestled
In between his birth and death dates.
But no matter how many times
We've been there
It takes several minutes
To find him.
I look over at the brick wall at the back of the plot
The walkway on the side
And count my way to him.
Finally there he is.
After pulling away
The errant blades of grass
And brushing specks of dirt covering him,
I leave a small smooth stone
To mark the little time with him that day.
Tragedy in Perspective

They say, poets need to retell the story.
Poets need to find meaning in the devastation,
the incineration of thousands. We are the ones
who are supposed to make the world feel better
with the beauty of our words.

But, I can't find the meaning.
All I see is the grief, the disbelief,
and the yearning, searching looks
on the relatives, friends, colleagues
who want to know why their loved ones
vanished so quickly – like they were sucked up
by a UFO, a tornado, an avalanche
never to be heard from or seen again.

Perhaps if I compare this devastation
to the one in my life
I can find the right words.
The day Paul took his life,
September 23, 1999,
my life and the lives of my family
were never the same again.
But, is it too selfish, too petty to look
at the Hamas-Israel war that way?

So, let me simply say,
I can relate to those left behind
and I can feel their pain.
I can tell them I've been there too.
I know what it feels like to have a beautiful
living, breathing human being reduced to
a bag of ashes.

The Wishing Dream

I startled and opened my eyes
wide in disbelief.
There was Paul
standing by my bed,
calm, quiet, his lips turned up in
the little smile I remembered so well.
I reached up to touch him.
His pale skin was cool, dry, and real.
Mom, I've come back.
I really didn't mean to leave forever
two years ago.
And as he spoke the tears began
pouring from my eyes
I was crying for all the days
I'd missed him, mourned him, looked for him.
How I scoured the faces of all the
blue-eyed young men
with short blonde hair
and black lashes who passed by.
How I listened for his music
every time I heard a jazz piano tune
in a bar, on the radio, on a CD.
How I remembered him everywhere I went –
under the Manhattan Beach pier,
on the wide, red-tiled stoop outside Starbucks,
at a dingy piano bar on Avenue A
in New York's lower east side,
in the kitchen munching on a handful of almonds,
sitting cross legged on the floor of his room

where his jazz records still stand
in ordered rows on the shelf.
I got up and went to him
and gave him a welcoming hug,
never wanting to let him go again.

Cat Stevens Then and Now

As I walked up the stairs I heard Cat Stevens singing
The familiar words of his song, "Morning has Broken,"
And there I was back in 1973
In our old gray Chrysler station wagon
With the wood trim and fake red leather seats
And Paul was sitting in the back
Belting out the words with him. He was only two then
Still clutching his green stuffed turtle for dear life
As we drove along.
His fat cheeks were rosy red, his blonde hair
Cut like an upside-down cereal bowl around his face.
Then I return to this day and my table at the
Westside Pavilion Mall where the lunch crowd
Is beginning to gather not knowing or caring how I grieve
For the chubby little boy sitting in his car seat
When so little made him happy.

Dream World

I walked into her hospital room and looked toward her bed. It was in a sunny spot by the window. A young nurse was with her, and they were smiling.

She was lying in the bed, wearing a light blue hospital gown covered with a tiny geometric print of triangles, squares and circles in shades of gray, burgundy and a dark blue.

Her skin looked healthy – a little pinkish – and her thin, stringy, almost white hair was carefully brushed off her face.

She seemed glad to see me, and as the nurse left, she looked at me with wide, bright eyes and asked, "Do you want to play bridge? We need a fourth."

I explained that I couldn't, hadn't played in years. She accepted that excuse as she looked from side to side.

She pointed her fingers with her long almond shaped painted nails to two or three others – people she imagined were in the room with her – and said they would play.

I stood by her bed, just looking at her, stroking her damp forehead and holding her bony hand – still very bruised from all the needles that had been stuck into her.

I brushed my fingers down her white, silky smooth legs – now because of her age – totally devoid of hair, and I realized that she was in her own private dream world. One that she had lived in maybe 60 to 70 years ago.

 I wasn't in it. Today, she didn't even know who I was.

"Do I look a mess?" she asked me. "No, you look wonderful," I said. She smiled up at me, not minding that her mouth was without her bottom dentures, and bragged that her cousins, Virginia and Cal, always told her how good she looked and how well-dressed she always was.

So, even in this hospital bed with her gown hiked up almost to her diaper, she cared about how she looked.

I tried to get her gown down, but she kept grabbing onto it. I covered her with a sheet and sat down and watched her for a while.

She surely wasn't interested in talking to me. She was too busy playing cards with her imaginary partners, while using her night gown as her bridge hand.

"Six spades," she proudly proclaimed and, looking in my direction, told me to play out. I made a playing out kind of gesture that she seemed satisfied with, and she continued picking at the material of her gown.

She was trying to lift off each pattern section one by one as if it were a playing card and place it on the imaginary table in front of her.

I asked for the nurse. I wanted to know what had happened to her. I wanted to know why she was so obviously out of her right mind today.

"Hospitalitis," the nurse said glibly – like she had seen this kind of behavior a million times before.

So, all I was left with was the hope that today's confusion would pass like it had when she had been hospitalized before.

In the meantime, I felt so helpless. I didn't know how to fix her, and I didn't think anyone else knew either. We were all just playacting along with her. And yet I was thankful too.

She seemed so happy. Her mind was taking her to another place – one where she was young and beautiful and full of life. Where she was back with her husband and her many relatives and friends on the west side of Chicago.

I hadn't seen her look so happy in years. "I like this little room," she told me. And I was glad.

Letting Go

She flexed her fists
on the cold bed railing
keeping in time
with the rhythm of her heartbeats.
Soon her hold relaxed,
and with fingers intertwined
she wrapped her hands around the bar.

Drugged from the morphine potion
placed under her tongue,
she lay in a ball like a sleeping skeleton,
her head tucked into her sunken chest.
I sat with her, stroked her arm
like a skinny rail itself
and soothed the damp hair off her forehead
until she pushed me away
and took hold the railing again.

Finally too weak to reach her metal friend,
she allowed her folder fingers
to rest on the bed.
And I, kissing her graying, fading face
said my last I love you and goodbye.
A woman strong until the end
took 94 years to finally let go.

Remembering Paul

I'll always remember that he slept without closing his eyes all the
way
I'll always remember that he walked fast and way ahead of us
I'll always remember that he had long, thick, black eyelashes
surrounding clear blue eyes
I'll always remember that he played the piano with legs crossed
at the knees, leaning way down over the keyboard
I'll always remember that he liked to wear second-hand clothes
and didn't mind if they were ripped
I'll always remember that he stood at the pantry door munching
almonds
I'll always remember that he liked to climb – trees, rocks, diving
boards
I'll always remember that he was meticulous and anal about his
things
I'll always remember that he could play almost any tune by ear

And that he was always a loner
And how much he loved his girlfriend and wasn't touched
enough after she left him

I'll always remember that he was sensitive
I'll always remember that he drove too fast and erratically
I'll always remember that he got lots of parking tickets
I'll always remember that he was in love with John Lennon
I'll always remember that he liked Doc Martin shoes
I'll always remember that he tapped his foot when he sat down
I'll always remember that he sat all folded over like The Thinker
when he drank coffee at Starbucks

I won't ever forget the feel of his cool pale skin the last night I
saw him
Or the sound of his voice
I'll always remember that his hair was very thick

I can't forget that he knew all the nursery rhymes by heart by
the time he was two And he said
He wanted to watch a record when he lay down on the red and
black plaid couch to take a nap
I'll always remember that he loved to fish
I'll always remember that he and his brother called the back of
the station wagon, "the really back"

I'll always remember that he loved New York until he got sick
Then he was afraid of it.
I can't remember how his hand felt in mine. Was it smooth, was
it rough?
And now I'll never know.